Olympic Greats

OLYMPIC GYMNASTICS LEGENDS

MARTIN GITLIN

BLACK
RABBIT
BOOKS

Bolt is published by Black Rabbit Books
P.O. Box 3263, Mankato, Minnesota, 56002.
www.blackrabbitbooks.com
Copyright © 2021 Black Rabbit Books

Jen Besel, editor; Catherine Cates, designer;
Omay Ayres, photo researcher

Library of Congress Cataloging-in-Publication Data
Names: Gitlin, Marty, author.
Title: Olympic gymnastics legends / by Martin Gitlin.
Other titles: Bolt (North Mankato, Minn.)
Description: Mankato, Minnesota : Bolt is published by Black Rabbit Books,
2021. | Series: Bolt. Olympic greats | Audience: Ages: 8-12 years. |
Audience: Grades: 4-6. Identifiers: LCCN 2019027607 (print) | ISBN 9781623102661
(Hardcover) | ISBN 9781644663622 (Paperback) | ISBN 9781623103606 (eBook)
Subjects: LCSH: Gymnasts—Juvenile literature. | Gymnastics—Records. |
Olympics—Juvenile literature.
Classification: LCC GV461.3 .G58 2021 (print) | LCC GV461.3 (ebook) |
DDC 796.44—dc23
LC record available at https://lccn.loc.gov/2019027607
LC ebook record available at https://lccn.loc.gov/2019027608

Printed in the United States. 2/20

All statistics are through the 2016 Olympic Games.

Image Credits
Alamy: ITAR-TASS News Agency,
Cover, 1, 19 (t); Jack Sullivan, 12, 17,
23, 28–29 (medal); Roger Sedres, 19 (b);
SPUTNIK, 26; Xinhua, 4–5; AP Images: AMY
SANCETTA, 22; ASSOCIATED PRESS, 15, 16; Craig
Fujii, 25 (cr); DIETER ENDLICHER, 25 (t); SANTI-
AGO LYON, 25 (cl); Getty: Colorado Springs Gazette,
10–11 (main); picture alliance, 6–7 (main); ullstein bild,
13 (main); Newscom: Zdenek Havelka/ZUMA Press, 12
(main); Shutterstock: Eugene Onischenko, 8–9 (bkgd);
kapona, 31; Luigi Fardella, 3, 32; Miceking, 8–9 (figures);
Nata-Art, 6, 13, 18, 20–21, 24 (medals); Paul Crash, 10,
14, 20, 27, 29 (rings); www.vssg.net: VSSG, 25 (b)
Every effort has been made to contact copyright
holders for material reproduced in this book.
Any omissions will be rectified in
subsequent printings if notice is
given to the publisher.

CONTENTS

Amazing

ATHLETES

They spin, jump, and dance. They leap high in the air and land on their feet. Gymnasts are powerful athletes. And the best compete in the Summer Olympics.

The Summer Games are held every four years. Countries send their best gymnasts to compete.

Powerful

PERFORMERS

Nikolai Andrianov

Nikolai Andrianov did not start in gymnastics until age 12. But he won Olympic gold less than eight years later. Andrianov pushed to be the best. He did triple backflips when others only did doubles. He won a medal in every men's event at least once.

COUNTRY	RUSSIA	
OLYMPIC YEARS	1972, 1976, 1980	
BRONZE MEDALS	SILVER MEDALS	GOLD MEDALS
3	5	7

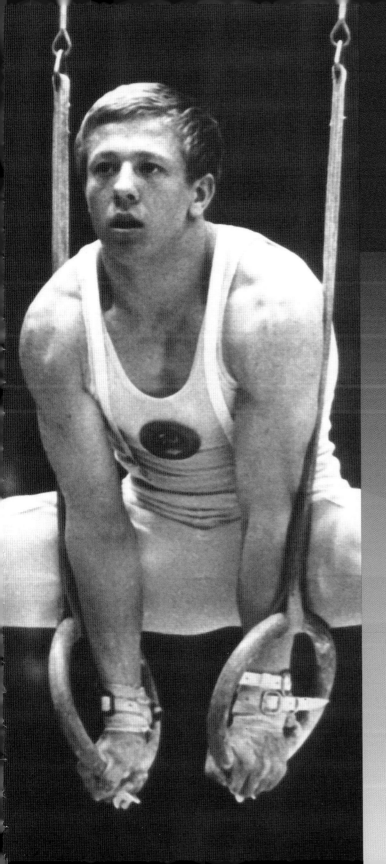

Top Olympic Medal Winners

28
Michael Phelps
(swimming)

18
Larisa Latynina
(gymnastics)

15
Nikolai Andrianov
(gymnastics)

13
Edoardo Mangiarotti
(fencing)

13
Takashi Ono
(gymnastics)

13
Boris Shakhlin
(gymnastics)

GYMNASTICS EVENTS

Gymnasts compete in different events. They can medal in each event. Athletes also compete in the all-around. Scores from each event are added together. Athletes with the highest overall scores win the all-around. Each country competes for team medals too.

PARALLEL BARS (men)

HORIZONTAL BAR (men)

FLOOR EXERCISES (men & women)

BALANCE BEAM (women)

VAULT

(men & women)

UNEVEN BARS

(women)

STILL RINGS

(men)

POMMEL HORSE

(men)

Simone Biles

Simone Biles **dominated** the 2016 Games. She won the floor exercise and vault. She also took gold in the individual all-around.

Biles has incredible skill and **form**. She does moves other gymnasts won't try.

COUNTRY
UNITED STATES

BRONZE MEDALS
1

GOLD MEDALS
4

2016 OLYMPIC YEARS

0
SILVER MEDALS

As of October 2019, Biles has four moves named after her.

Vera Caslavska

Many people say Vera Caslavska changed gymnastics forever. Before her, the sport was focused on dance moves. She gave it a more **athletic** style. Her powerful moves earned her 11 Olympic medals. Two of them were all-around golds.

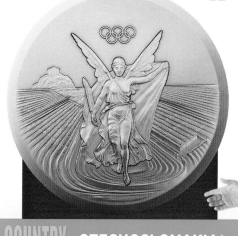

COUNTRY	CZECHOSLOVAKIA*

OLYMPIC YEARS	1960, 1964, 1968

BRONZE MEDALS	SILVER MEDALS	GOLD MEDALS
0	4	7

Viktor Chukarin

Viktor Chukarin was one of the greatest gymnasts of his time. He won the all-around gold in 1952 and 1956.

Chukarin was a **prisoner** during World War II. He nearly starved. But he survived. And he went on to win 11 medals.

COUNTRY	SOVIET UNION*
OLYMPIC YEARS	1952, 1956

BRONZE MEDALS	SILVER MEDALS	GOLD MEDALS
1	3	7

*Czechoslovakia and the Soviet Union no longer exist.

Nadia Comaneci

Nadia Comaneci was the star of the 1976 Games. She earned the first perfect score in Olympic history. She earned a perfect 10 in the uneven bars. She got perfect scores six more times during those Games.

COUNTRY
ROMANIA

BRONZE
MEDALS
1

GOLD
MEDALS
5

1976, 1980
OLYMPIC YEARS

3
SILVER
MEDALS

Comaneci weighed about
85 pounds (39 kilograms) at the 1976 Games.

Sawao Kato

Sawao Kato began his Olympic **career** strong. He won three gold medals in his first Games. He was especially strong on the parallel bars. Kato won that event in both 1972 and 1976. But he was great in all events. He medaled in the all-around in all his Olympic Games.

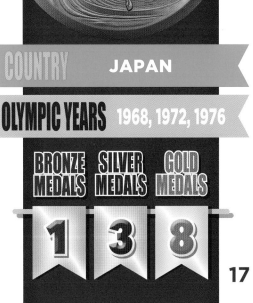

COUNTRY **JAPAN**

OLYMPIC YEARS 1968, 1972, 1976

BRONZE MEDALS SILVER MEDALS GOLD MEDALS

1 3 8

Larisa Latynina

Larisa Latynina won more medals than any other Olympic gymnast. She had great form. She made few mistakes. Her strongest event might have been the floor. She won gold in that event at all three Olympics.

COUNTRY **SOVIET UNION**

OLYMPIC YEARS 1956, 1960, 1964

BRONZE MEDALS 4   SILVER MEDALS 5   GOLD MEDALS 9

Latynina held the record for most Olympic medals for nearly 50 years. Swimmer Michael Phelps · · · broke her record in 2012.

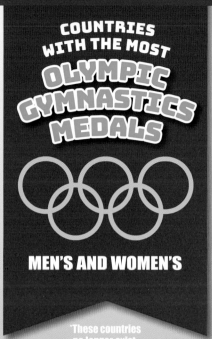

COUNTRIES WITH THE MOST OLYMPIC GYMNASTICS MEDALS

MEN'S AND WOMEN'S

Country	Gold Medals Won
Germany	14
East Germany*	6
Hungary	15
Russia	10
Switzerland	16
China	
Romania	
Japan	
United States	
Soviet Union*	

GOLD MEDALS WON   0   10

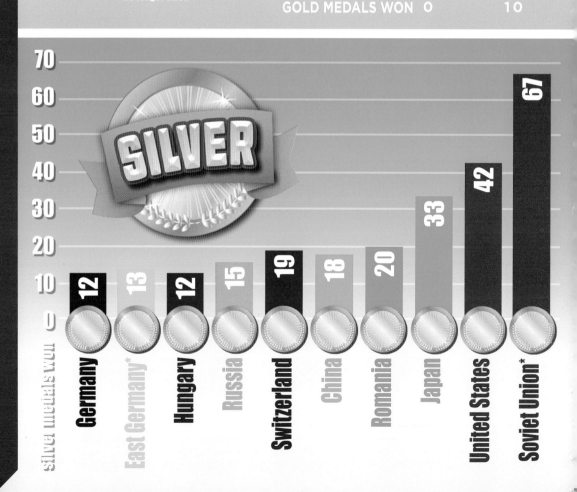

SILVER

silver medals won

Country	Silver Medals
Germany	12
East Germany*	13
Hungary	12
Russia	15
Switzerland	19
China	18
Romania	20
Japan	33
United States	42
Soviet Union*	67

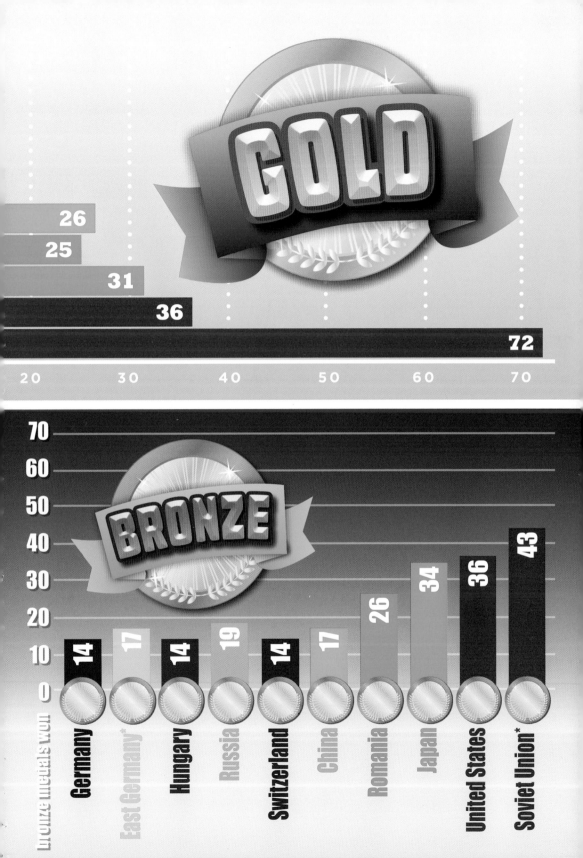

GOLD

	26
	25
	31
	36
	72

20   30   40   50   60   70

BRONZE

70
60
50
40
30
20
10
0

Country	Bronze
Germany	14
East Germany*	17
Hungary	14
Russia	19
Switzerland	14
China	17
Romania	26
Japan	34
United States	36
Soviet Union*	43

bronze medals won

Alexei Nemov

Alexei Nemov was a fan favorite. People loved his strength and style. In his first Games, he led Russia to its first team title. After his first Games, he had a shoulder injury. But that didn't stop him. In his career, he won 12 Olympic medals.

COUNTRY **RUSSIA**

OLYMPIC YEARS 1996, 2000, 2004

BRONZE MEDALS	SILVER MEDALS	GOLD MEDALS
6	2	4

Vitaly Scherbo

August 2, 1992, was a record day. That day, Vitaly Scherbo won four gold medals. He was the first to win that many in one day.

Scherbo was known for his moves. He was also known for his **personality**. He hated losing. When he didn't like something, he let the judges know.

COUNTRY BELARUS

OLYMPIC YEARS 1992, 1996

BRONZE MEDALS 4   SILVER MEDALS 0   GOLD MEDALS 6

FOUR GOLDS IN ONE DAY

POMMEL HORSE

RINGS

PARALLEL BARS

VAULT

Boris Shakhlin

Boris Shakhlin was calm and steady. He was nicknamed "Man of Iron." He once said his favorite moment was in the 1960 Games. And it wasn't a gold medal win. His **grip** came off on the horizontal bar. His hand began bleeding. But he completed his **routine** anyway.

COUNTRY SOVIET UNION

1956, 1960, 1964 OLYMPIC YEARS

BRONZE MEDALS 2

4 SILVER MEDALS

GOLD MEDALS 7

CHAPTER 3

Comparing

CAREERS

Gymnasts push to be the best during the Summer Olympics. Compare the stats of some of Olympic gymnastics' greatest.

TOTAL MEDALS

NUMBER OF MEDALS

20
18
16
15
13
12
12
12
8
4
0

Larisa Latynina   **Nikolai Andrianov**   **Boris Shakhlin**   **Sawao Kato**   **Alexei Nemov**

OLYMPIC APPEARANCES

Name	Number of Olympic Appearances
Simone Biles	1
Viktor Chukarin	2
Nadia Comaneci	2
Vitaly Scherbo	2
Nikolai Andrianov	3
Vera Caslavska	3
Sawao Kato	3
Larisa Latynina	3
Alexei Nemov	3
Boris Shakhlin	3

NUMBER OF OLYMPIC APPEARANCES

0   1   2   3

11	11	10	9	5
Vera Caslavska	Viktor Chukarin	Vitaly Scherbo	Nadia Comaneci	Simone Biles

athletic (ahth-LEH-tik)—focused on strength and power

career (kuh-REER)—a period of time spent in a job

dominate (DOM-uh-neyt)—to hold a commanding position over

form (FORM)—a manner or style of performing

grip (GRIHP)—a device worn by gymnasts on bars or rings; they help protect the hands.

personality (per-suh-NA-lah-te)—the set of qualities that makes a person or animal different from others

prisoner (PRI-zuh-nur)—someone who has been captured or locked up

routine (ROO-teen)—a series of things that are repeated as part of a performance

BOOKS

Herman, Gail. *What Are the Summer Olympics?* What Are …? New York: Grosset & Dunlap, an imprint of Penguin Random House, 2016.

Schlegel, Elfi, and Claire Ross Dunn. *The Gymnastics Book: The Young Performer's Guide to Gymnastics.* New York: Firefly Books, 2018.

Sherman, Jill. *Simone Biles.* Pro Sport Biographies. Mankato, MN: Amicus/Amicus Ink, 2020.

WEBSITES

Gymnastics Artistic
www.olympic.org/gymnastics-artistic

Nadia Comaneci – First Perfect 10
www.youtube.com/watch?v=Yi_5xbd5xdE

USA Gymnastics | Gymnastics 101
usagym.org/pages/gymnastics101/

INDEX